GOD, WHY CORONA?

DISCERNING GOD'S REASON FOR THE PANDEMIC

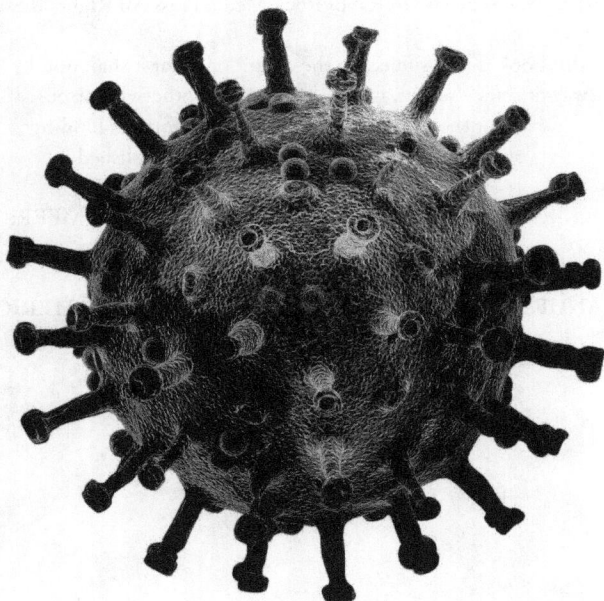

SHAUL & NOAH PRAVER

LIBRARY OF CONGRESS CATALOG CARD NUMBER:
ISBN 978-1-7343595-2-7

MANUFACTURED IN THE UNITED STATES OF AMERICA

AUTHORS' FOREWORD

This is an extraordinarily difficult time for the entire world. At this very moment 1,199,064 people have tested positive for the Corona Virus, 64,650 people have died from it and 246,166 have recovered from it. It is Saturday night, April 4, 2020. As I co-wrote this book with my son Noah by transcribing some of our recent Socratic dialogues, I cannot be certain if I myself, God forbid, will wind up in any one of these three categories of statistics. As a prison chaplain still working on the front lines, I am taking every reasonable precaution to protect my own life and not infect my family members. Noah's probing philosophical nature has been the inspiration behind this volume. His uncle Sholom Praver, himself an avid student of the Talmud and Judaic tradition, has proven to be a talented and inspiring editor who has done much to improve this project.

This reflection is written as an answer to one simple question. Assuming God brought the Coronavirus to our planet, why would God do it? Some have responded with great anger at this question and even more so, to the answers we've provided. They hear in the question and the answers, a lack of compassion and empathy for the people who are suffering and died from Coronavirus. We were puzzled by this response, but we have given it a lot of thought and decided to add this Authors' Foreword to address those concerns before readers proceed into the book.

By asking the question it doesn't mean we lack empathy or compassion for those who are suffering or died. Members of our own family are at great risk and the opposite is the case. We have tremendous love, compassion and empathy for every person and the entire planet. We are inspired by the words of Victor Frankl a holocaust survivor and author of Man's Search for Meaning, who said, "He who has a <u>why</u> to live can bear almost any <u>how</u> (to live)." We are trying to discern the <u>why</u> behind Corona, so people can find the <u>how</u> to overcome it.

In accordance with our Judaic faith, particularly at a time of calamity,[1] we are commanded to do T'shuvah,[2] to investigate our sins and repent. As it is said in Lamentations, "We will search and examine our ways, and return to the Omnipresent."[3] And in that spirit, we are stretching forth our hands to the Omnipresent and exclaiming, "We are here before You, what is it that You want of us? What actions do You demand of us so this plague may be removed from the planet? Will You have mercy upon us? Will You please, "Pardon, our iniquity and sin."[4] We long for You to answer us with these words, "I pardon you as you have asked."[5] We long for the Coronavirus to be over!

With these forewords in place, we hope our readers will discover some meaning in these difficult times. And we pray this meaning provides comfort and guidance in the days ahead.

---

[1] Talmud, Berachot, 5a

[2] Nachmanides cites two verses as sources for the mitzvah of T'shuva. Deuteronomy 4:30 "...you shall return to the Lord your G-d...", and Deuteronomy 30:1, "And you shall return to your heart..."

[3] Lamentations, 3:40

[4] Exodus, 34:9

[5] Numbers, 14:37

PREFACE

By addressing this subject of God's jurisprudence in this short reflection, I have taken on one of the thorniest theological questions that perplexed countless theologians and philosophers since the dawn of human history. Kind Abraham asked God why God was destroying the righteous along with the wicked;[6] innocent Job suffered great affliction for no apparent reason; and now, tens of thousands of kind and innocent people deeply loved by their families, were swept away by Coronavirus for no apparent reason. So many of us are left feeling sad, shocked and confused.

And yet, our tradition asks us to grapple with the words of prophet Isaiah,[7] "I form light and create darkness; I make peace and create evil— I, the LORD, do all these things." It is hard to make sense of it, and particularly when it involves innocent victims, we all fail. It is beyond our capacity to accept emotionally or intellectually. Most of us give up. But we must never give up!

I believe Prophet Isaiah asked us to consider that God's thoughts are not our thoughts[8] and if we knew more, we might be able to understand. It is not that God creates evil Himself, but by granting humankind free will, inevitably the capacity for human evil is created alongside free will. Those who believe that Coronavirus was either intentionally inflicted upon us by God or that God allowed it to occur through natural means, are struggling and deeply humbled. How are we to respond?

In Judaism, when calamity strikes, we respond with prayers, lamentations and repentance. Even if we do not understand why

---

[6] **Genesis 18:25** "Far be it from you to do such a thing-**to kill the** righteous **with** the wicked, treating the righteous and **the wicked** alike. Far be it from you! Will not the Judge of all the earth do, right?"

[7] Isaiah, 45:7

[8] Isaiah, 55:8

we are praying and repenting, we do it anyway.[9] We reason, this is how we've been instructed in the Torah and it never hurts to look within ourselves as individuals and as a society, to discover ways we can improve. When we do this, we inevitably draw closer to God, the source of life and wisdom. We also honor our Neshama, Godly Soul[10] and we honor the sacred memory of the victims. This response also gives us time and space to grieve.

But prayer and repentance must never be in lieu of social distancing, wearing masks and gloves, washing our hands and all other appropriate protective measures. Please look at the picture below. What do you see? Figure it out for yourself before you read on.

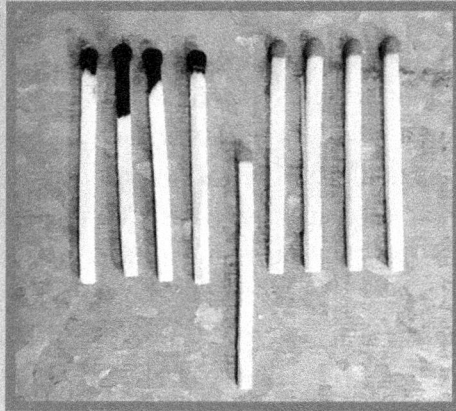

The one that stayed away, [social distanced] saved itself and all the rest.

---

[9] "At the moment when the Jewish people said **first 'We will do' and then 'We will understand**,' [Exodus 24:7] a heavenly voice went out and said to them, Who revealed to my children this secret, employed by the angels, as it is written, 'Praise God, O God's angels, mighty in strength, who **do** God's **will** and <u>understand</u> God's word '"(Tractate Shabbat 88a). Our actions are not predicated on our understanding, our understanding is predicated on our actions. To truly understand there must be a mixture of action followed by reflection. Insights are more inspired by actions than actions are inspired by insights.
[10] There are three types of souls in Humankind like a rope with three strands. Nefesh, Ruach and Neshama. The Nefesh is the physical soul of the human body which is shared by the animal kingdom. Whereas, Neshama and Ruach are unique to humankind. The Ruach is influenced by the Nefesh below it and the Neshama above it. This bundle of three souls is what makes humankind made in the Divine image. The human personality can choose to be influenced primarily by their Neshama and rise to great states of being.

When God "social distanced," through a process of Ztimtzum,[11] the universe was formed and continues forming in that space of concealment. When we practice social distancing, we mirror God's act of concealment and prevent the world from being burned up in an unbridled fire. But there is a paradox lurking that must be named. On the one hand God conceals Himself to make space for the universe to exist, and on the other hand we are enjoined to discover God in the universe. If God wants us to discover him, why does he hide?

If God revealed Himself by immediately punishing humankind for every evil act, we would not have free will because we would instantly know we cannot prosper in our evil.[12] The entire process of discovering and obeying God's will and discerning the reality of karma (measure for measure) is our very life purpose! It's a Divine game of Hide-and-Go-Seek and God wants to be found! When we obey God, we discover God. And if God did not conceal the full measure of His light, we could not exist autonomously. We would be immediately consumed in God's infinite light. God's act of concealment enables the universe to exist and for humankind to earn a unique place in eternity. If it was easy to understand all this, the reward wouldn't be worth so much.

In conclusion, we must obey the "commandments," as clearly outlined by authorities[13] in our state and federal agencies; they are good and correct in the rules they've prescribed. We must also pay attention to important lessons God is trying to teach us. The importance of nurturing our families, relating to the earth as a living vibrant being, respecting the elderly and all vulnerable people in society; being charitable; taking care of each other and valuing spirituality. With these core lessons learned, we grow closer to God and

---

[11] The tzimtzum is a Hebrew term used in the Lurianic Kabbalah to explain Isaac Luria's doctrine that God began the process of creation by "contracting" his Ohr Ein Sof (infinite light) in order to allow for a "conceptual space" in which finite and seemingly independent realms could exist.

[12] Be'ar Mayim Chayim, Talmud Berachot

[13] Dina d'malchuta dina, the law of the state is the law and is to be regarded as binding upon Jews as a religious duty of the Torah.

our neighbors. And while we can't understand why so many kind and innocent people were swept out of the world by Coronavirus, we can work together to make the world a better place. We can work to make the planet safer and much better prepared for future viruses so that they don't grow into worldwide pandemics.

Stay safe. Stay healthy. Keep learning and always be blessed.

DISCLAIMER

The authors are not prophets nor the sons of prophets.[14] The work is a creative piece that attempts to discern The Omnipresent's will and message for Humankind and the planet during the Coronavirus pandemic. The opinions expressed in this work do not represent the opinions of any other individual, group, department, agency, house of worship or organization of any kind. The opinions represent only the views of the authors.

---

[14] Amos, 7:14

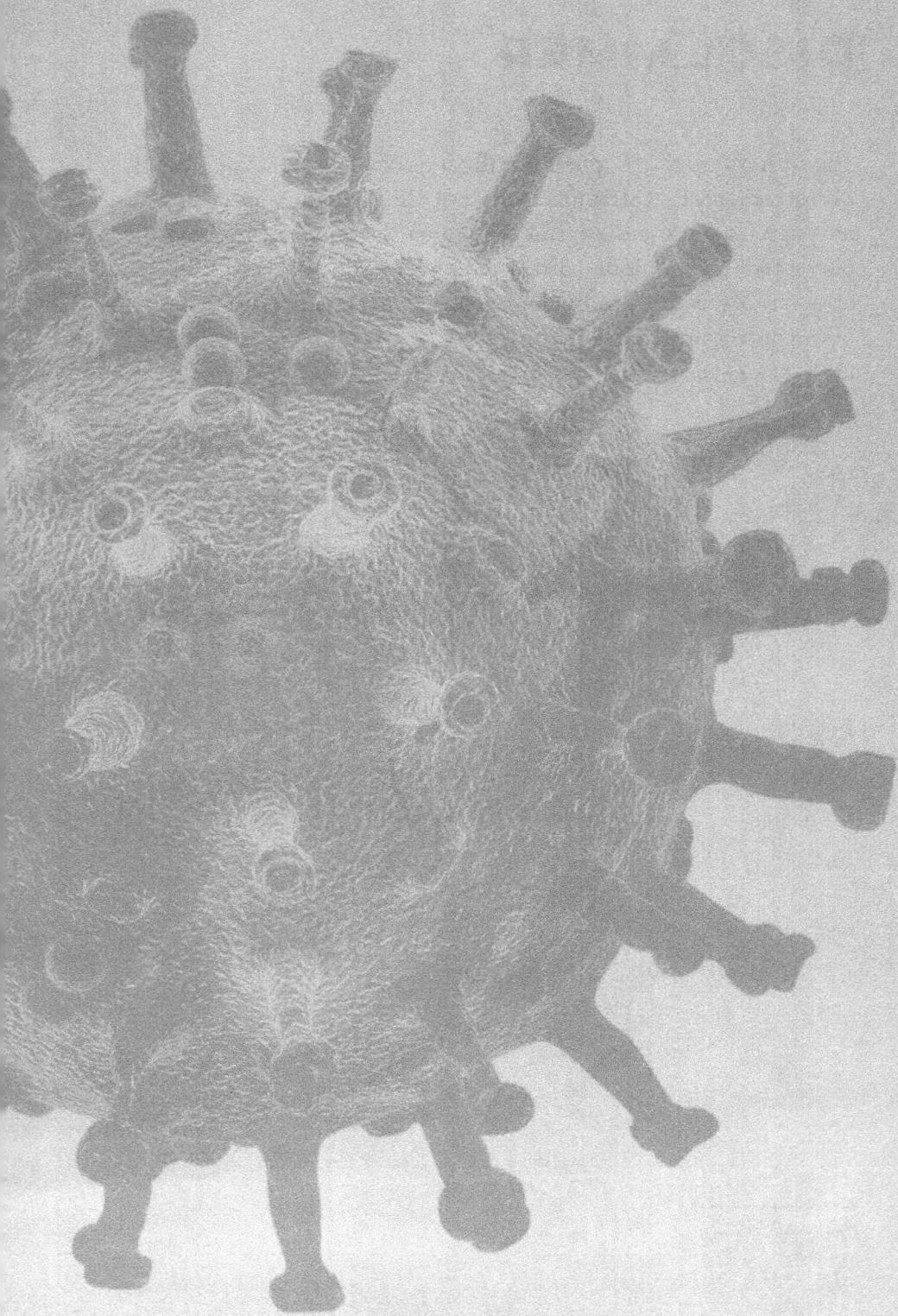

GOD, WHY CORONAVIRUS?

Because of My abundance of love for humankind I have visited upon you the Coronavirus. I know many of you are hurting and scared. That is why I sent you this letter. I want you to know I am with you now in your shock and fear. I am with you when you are sick and suffering. I am with you when you are concluding your earthly sojourn. I wish I could show you the beautiful world of eternity that awaits you, but I can't.[15] It is something you must learn and earn for yourself. Eventually you will see in the midst of the

---

[15] Talmud Brachot 34b, "The Gemara asks: What is this reward about which it is said: "No eye has seen it"? Rabbi Yehoshua ben Levi said: That is the wine that has been preserved in its grapes since the six days of creation and which no eye has ever seen. Rabbi Shmuel bar Naḥmani said: That is Eden, which no creature's eye has ever surveyed." (And that is the reward and bliss we shall be shown in the world to come.)

darkness, My love shining through you. Then you will know that you live in Me forever and all is good.

As parents, you've had to visit upon your children discipline to protect them from their own recklessness. You did this out of the abundance of love you have for them. You allowed your children to learn and discover life for themselves, but you intervened when their lives depended upon it.

But, so many of you stopped being close and loving families. The Coronavirus created the conditions for you to become that kind of family again. Parents are seen and heard playing with their children in the yard, joggers are everywhere, children are riding their bicycles and the sound of laughter is heard in neighborhoods throughout the world again. You may wonder why the family is so important to Me. Each family is like one cell in the body of humankind. If the family is healthy, humankind is healthy. The family is where you learn to love and care for each other. It is where you learn about respect and empathy. Without love, respect and empathy humankind would destroy itself. When we focus on loving our family members, we prepare ourselves to extend that circle of love out into the community much more than we have before.

You are all home schooling now and restoration of the family is one of the big lessons you are learning. Friends are wonderful, but the nucleus of your lives was always meant to be your family. Many of you are fortunate to have a loving strong family and others may have had to form a new family because of dysfunction in their family of origins. And there are times when you are away from your family for an extended period and you need to form a family away from home with whom you belong. There are all kinds of families. What they all have in common are roots that support all other loving relationships that branch out throughout your lives.

GOD, ARE THERE OTHER THINGS YOU WANT TO CORRECT IN HUMANITY WITH THE CORONAVIRUS?

Yes. You were destroying the earth as a living, vibrant and luminous being. You kept talking about fixing it but failed to organize and get it done. You forgot that not only does humankind need a Sabbath to rejuvenate itself, the earth also needs a Sabbath[16] to rejuvenate herself. I forced you to give the earth a Sabbath and it didn't take long for blue skies to return over China and for the fish and dolphins to return to the canals in Venice, Italy. The earth was crying for a Sabbatical. Giving the planet a Sabbatical means stopping industry from time to time so the earth, sea and sky can rest and rejuvenate. The planet needs a Sabbath. You must treat My earth that I gave you as a living, vibrant luminous being, because, it is! You are smart enough to figure out how to institute a Sabbath for the planet while maintaining needed levels of production. But

---

[16] Leviticus 25:4, While the Sabbath for the Land is unique to The Land of Israel, its ecological benefits are universally relevant to all lands. Yet, environmental discourse rarely invokes such a simple and elegant solution. Indeed, we say, the Earth is a living, vibrant and luminous being that has a right to her Sabbatical.

it is not intelligence you are lacking; it is the love and good will to one another and nations that is lacking for global covenants to be established.

You must learn to consume less and appreciate the things you already have. You must observe the Sabbath. When you observe the Sabbath you learn to find meaning within yourself and the simple pleasures of life such as taking a walk, singing a song, telling stories, enjoying a home cooked meal, praying, studying, meditating, curling up with a book, telling jokes and simply laughing. You must do these things first with your families and then include some friends. Then go with all your families to a house of worship or the great outdoors near you and meet other families there. You should invite them to your home to eat and celebrate the Sabbath and other joyous occasions. You are home now to relearn the value of all these things. It's not just the children who are home schooling, it's the parents! Because you refused to establish a Sabbath for yourselves, I have imposed an extended Sabbath upon you. You are people of many walks of life and keeping my Sabbath is necessary for each family. Each in accordance with your faith and individual traditions. And for those who have no family, you must reach out to them and include them from time to time in your Sabbaths.

Children, you complained about going to school and said you preferred to be on your phone and other electronic devices. Now, the only way you can attend school is through an electronic device. Today, all you want is to be able to go back to school and be with your friends and teachers. You are so bored of going to school on a computer. I understand you completely. Do you see why you should stop complaining about school? Going to school is a beautiful thing. It's time to start appreciating it much more!

Respect for your elders. You are supposed to show respect for your elders,[17] but you have discarded the elderly and failed to value and care for them properly. Because they are the ones who are most vulnerable, you have been directed to think about them and their predicament much more these days. Until now, you have valued people based upon how much goods and services they are able to produce and not upon who they are as people. Since the elderly no longer work and produce goods and services, you have disrespected them. You have neglected the spiritual aspects of your own lives in favor of materialistic interests and you are striving after the wind.[18] You are so busy producing more and more, you forgot your purpose in life. You are a Human being not a human doing! You have lost your very soul and have valued only the things you can touch and feel.

Your intrinsic worth is found in your inner being, your thoughts, feelings, perceptions and consciousness. Your soul is who you really are, and it is your soul that lives on through eternity not your body or the goods and services you produced in this world. What you do

[17] Leviticus 19:32
[18] Ecclesiastes 1:14

is an important expression of your soul, but your soul is who you are and where your true worth is found. Many people have never learned this basic lesson and if they once learned it, they forgot. Now is the time to remember.

GOD, WHAT THEN IS OUR PURPOSE?

All I want of you is to be just, merciful and humble."[19] You have lost the ability to speak with each other respectfully. Today, human discourse lacks justice, mercy and humility. I have sent the virus to the most powerful and the least powerful to remind all of human-kind that you are mortal and delicate like the flower of the field. The wind passes over it and it is gone.[20] If you would only think first about the honor of your friend before your own honor, you

[19] Mica 6:8
[20] Psalms, 103:16

would fix a great deal within yourself.[21] If you would only try to understand the heart of your neighbor more than trying to refute and defeat your neighbor, you would come much closer to your purpose. You have not been put in this world to hate and destroy but to love and care for one another. Through love you will discover your true purpose.[22]

Humankind is interconnected through the internet, international banking and the flow of people, germs, and viruses more than any time in history. China is not some "other" place, nor are places like America, Europe, Africa or Australia some "other" place. You are all in the same place and that place is planet earth. I have created a magnificent living, vibrant, luminous planet for you.

---

[21] Pirke Avot, 4:1
[22] Jerimiah,9:24

What happens in one region of the world will eventually affect all other regions of the world. The Coronavirus dramatically demonstrates how all of humankind is interconnected. You have been living in the delusion that national boundaries are more than lines on a map. Even your walls do not prevent the spread of the virus. If humankind is going to continue existing on earth, you must cooperate with one another. Sworn enemies must forget their conflicts because now there is a common enemy bigger than these conflicts.

One person is not entitled to drill a hole on the bottom of his or her side of the boat. You are all in the same boat! You are interdependent and have responsibilities to one another on all points of the globe. Viruses, germs, hurricanes, tornadoes, heat waves, earthquakes, droughts, floods, mud slides and volcanic eruptions do not obey national borders but abide with interplanetary conditions that pay no regard to religions, cultures, languages, ethnicities or governments. When the boat sinks, everyone sinks!

How will you remember the core lessons I am trying to teach you? If you fail to consider the message, I will have to bring an even more severe set of circumstances to force you to comply with My will. The earth will have her Sabbaths with or without you.[23] What I am asking you to do is within your ability. You must understand that the earth that I gave you is a living, vibrant and luminous planet that you must learn to respect. Previous generations have been tested and learned to retain these core lessons. Each of you can take these lessons to heart and allow the experience to make its indelible mark. If most people respond in this way, collectively you will make a lasting change to world culture.

---

[23] Leviticus, 26:33-35

Your parents and grandparents who experienced the great depression in the 1930's changed world culture, you can too. Because of them, many more people have learned to appreciate what they have and practice conservation. You too can be forever transformed as a result of enduring this pandemic. I know you are currently experiencing shock and denial, but make no mistake about it, this is a game changer. It is the long overdue intervention that will correct several distortions and imbalances outlined in this letter. It is now up to you to make sure the core lessons of the Coronavirus make its positive impact upon you, your family, your community and the planet. What will you do to transmit the important lessons to your children and your peers? That is for each of you to figure out and put into action.

Now do you understand that what happens on one side of the world eventually spreads to the other side of the world? Now do you understand that you can only hold off certain planetary conditions from spreading across borders for a limited amount of time? Now do you understand that the earth is a living, vibrant and luminous being that must be granted her Sabbaths?

I will always reward those who work hard; those among you who have good ideas and implement them. But every society has its share of people who cannot provide for themselves. You must not discard them; they are your brothers and sisters. I have already instructed you to leave the corner of your field for those less fortunate than you.[24] When I blessed you for your labors under the sun, I also expected you to share your bounty and blessings with those who are not as blessed. This is what I mean by walking humbly with Me, having mercy upon one another and seeking justice in the world. These things I tell you are not beyond you to carry out. They are in your heart to do. My message is not a complicated message. It is very simple. It is about maintaining balance on the planet and preserving humankind. Your acts of Loving Kindness to one another preserve My divine image in you. My divine image is how I created you. I have encrypted inside you the will to be like Me and to practice loving kindness. When you go against My nature, My nature eventually goes against you. It's the reality of My creation. You must yield to My laws and governance.

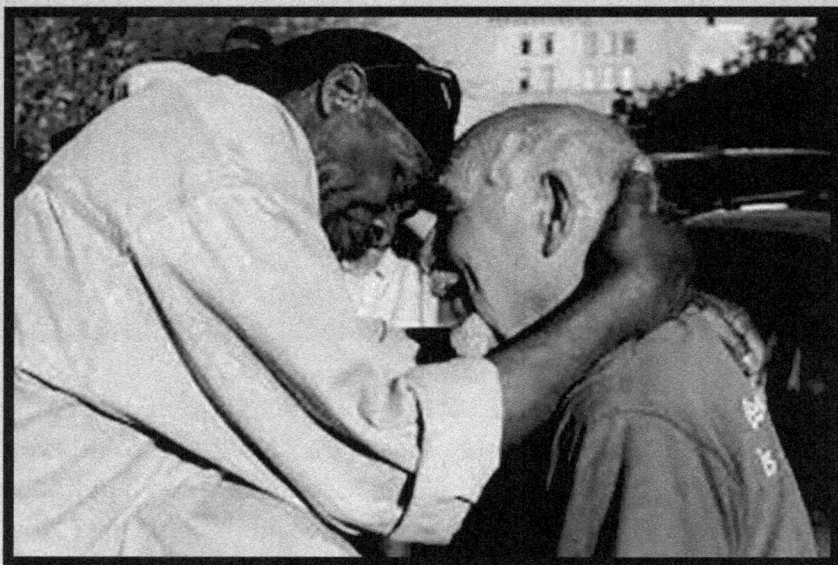

---

[24] Leviticus 22:23

It gives Me no pleasure to send you this virus and I cry with you when it takes the lives of the elderly, the weak and people of all ages. I created you with free will and you bring about much of these conditions on earth yourselves. But I have also given you the intelligence to solve your problems. Wake up! Arise! Hear my message today! You must adopt to these new circumstances. Because you failed to understand these things, you placed the life of humankind in jeopardy and you forced Me to intervene. Out of My abundant loving kindness for you, I have intervened in a way that brings about the least amount of death and suffering while delivering the greatest amount of transformation to human societies. There is no way you could have known what would have happened if I didn't send the Coronavirus. How could you have known that you were truly dangerously close to a catastrophic end to humankind? All I ask you to do is live up to your name, "Humankind." Be the kind of humans that are kind. Don't be divided by the kinds of humans that you are but be united by the kindness that defines you in My image. And when you carry out loving kindness to one another and the earth, sea and sky, My spirit shall reside with you. That is when you will come to know My true nature. That is when you shall come to realize that My image is not a physical form but of pure spirit.

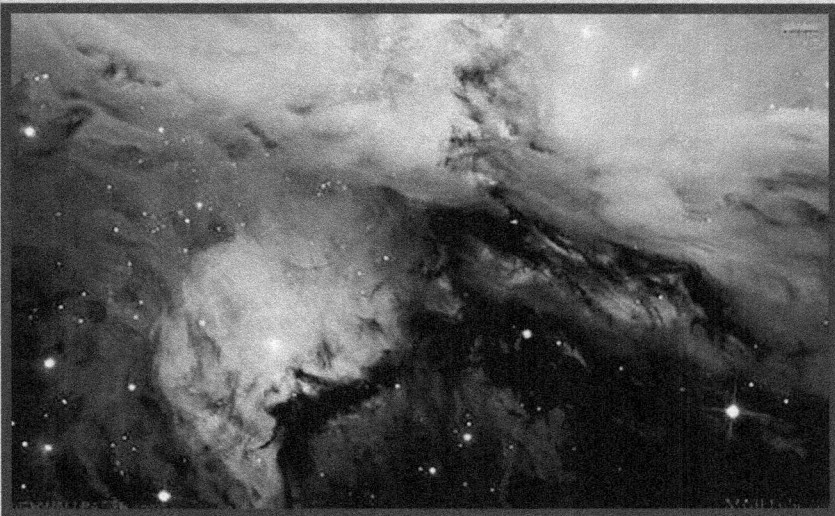

I am the Spirit and invisible thread that brought all things into existence and I continue enabling all things to exist. I never began, I always was, and I will always be. The way I live in you is by inspiring you to live before Me in accordance with My nature. As I am kind, you too be kind. As I am compassionate, you too be compassionate.[25] These are the simple things I am asking you to do. And when you do them as I have described in this letter, you will make yourselves and the earth new again. Then My abundant blessings shall be upon you and the earth, and you shall know peace.

---

[25] Talmud, Abba Shaul

SHAUL & NOAH PRAVER

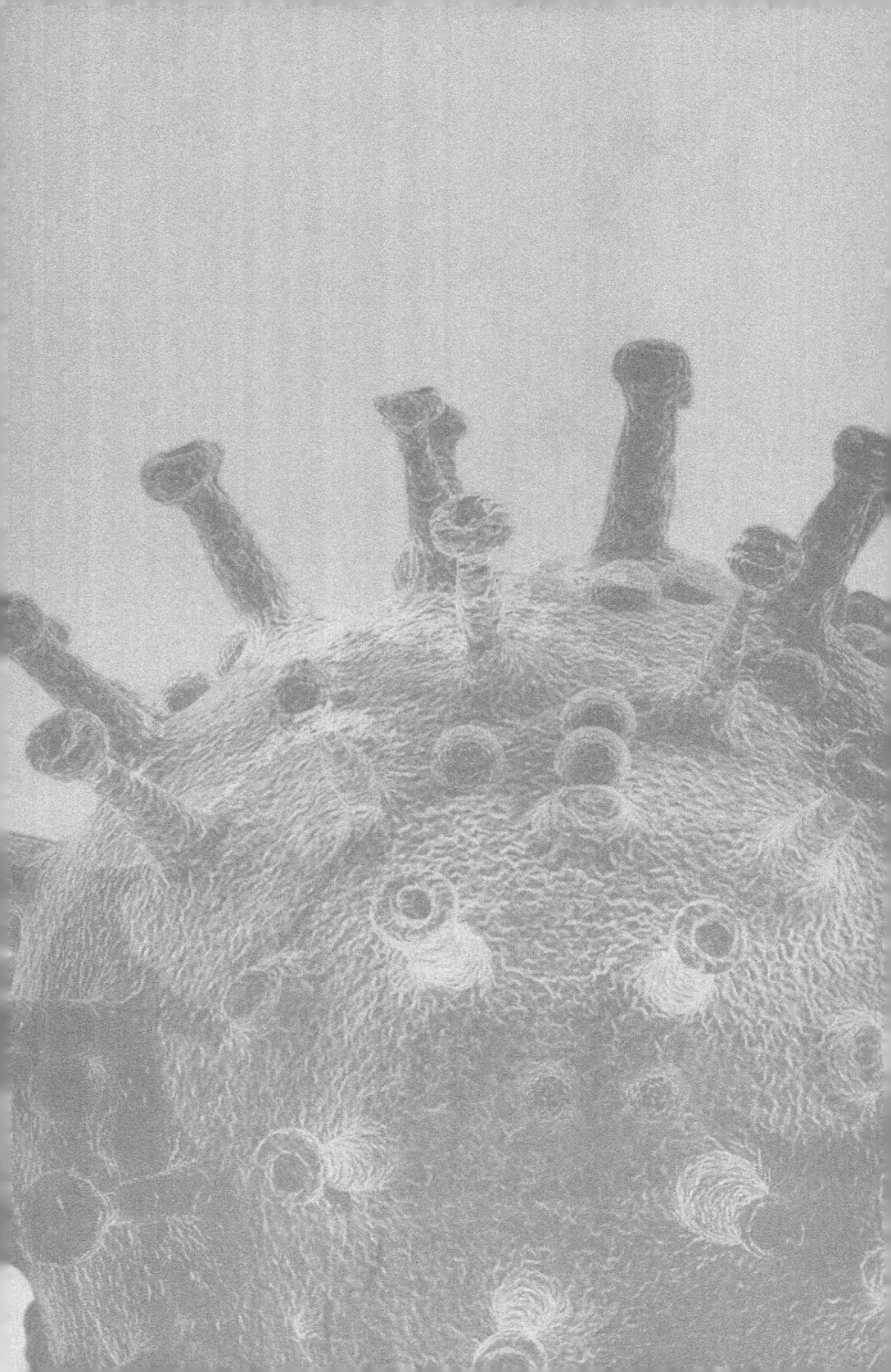

www.ingramcontent.com/pod-product-compliance
Lightning Source LLC
Chambersburg PA
CBHW020450030426
42337CB00014B/1486